Your First Condo

a reference handbook

Geoffrey D. Darwent

Disclaimer

The information contained in this guide should in no way be considered legal advice. Whenever real estate transactions are performed a competent attorney should be consulted.

First Edition

© Copyright 2014, Geoffrey Darwent. All rights reserved. Printed in Canada. This book may not be reproduced, either in part or in its entirety, in any form, by any means, without written permission from the author and or publisher, with the exception of brief excerpts for purposes of radio, television, or published review. Although all possible measures have been taken to ensure the accuracy of the material presented, neither the author nor the publisher is liable in case of misinterpretation and including directions, misapplication, or typographical error. All rights, including the right of translation, are reserved. No part of this publication may be reproduced, stored in or introduced into a retrieval system, or transmitted, in any form, or by means without the prior written permission of the Author. This book is sold subject to the condition that it shall not, by way of trade or otherwise, be lent, resold, hired out, or otherwise circulated without the Author's prior consent in any form of binding or cover other than that in which it is published and without a similar condition including the condition being imposed on the subsequent purchaser. Any resemblance to actual persons, living or dead is purely coincidental.

YOUR FIRST CONDO

To my sons Carlo and Adrian

Contents

- Snap Shot
- Who does the book benefit?
- To condo, or not to condo? That is the question
- The a-s-s in assuming
- Insurance
- The Condominium Association, Board of Directors and co-owners
- Okay! So who is responsible for what?
- Should I rent or should I own?
- Conditions to seller when buying
- Does the Manager's hat really fit?
- Other stuff

Snap Shot

A condominium or condo, is a type of real estate ownership which consists of both commonly owned and privately owned areas. The Co-Owners Association is the collective body formed by the constituent owners of a condominium. Apart from the Condominium's Governing Documents, each Condominium Association has a set of Bylaws that comprise a set of additional regulations and procedures that govern the internal operation of the condominium organization.

The Association's Board of Directors is a group of elected co-owners charged with the responsibility of operating and insuring the overall welfare of the condominium complex and, the Director who is a condominium owner, is elected by the association in order to contribute to the actions of the Board. The Board may then create a Committee and recruit a person or group of persons appointed to study, investigate and form a recommendation on specific issues. The Association may decide to hire a Management Company under contract in order to aid in the operation of the condominium complex.

The Association's insurance policy, unlike the co-owners' insurance policy which protects the individual owner's property, provides protection for the common elements of the condominium complex and is paid for by an insurance premium which is a sum of money paid to maintain insurance coverage.

Every Association will have an Annual General Meeting which is a meeting of all co-owners in a condominium usually held at the end of the association's fiscal year. The association's Fiscal Year End is comprised of a twelve month period in which a complete accounting is done. Depending on the association and the complexity involved, an annual audit may be required. An audit provides an examination, by a designated Chartered Accountant, of the association's financial records.

The meeting should use the Robert's Rules of Order which is an established procedure for conducting a meeting. For a matter of record, the Minutes of the meeting are taken; this is a written transcript or summary of a meeting. Should it be impossible for a co-owner to attend the Annual General Meeting, he or she can submit a Proxy in the form of a person or document that acts on behalf of the absentee co-owner. Once the President of the Board brings the meeting to order, a quorum must be determined.

A Quorum is the number of members of a group that must be present in order to legally transact business.

The Board of Directors must have a Budget and / or a financial plan which projects the future expenses and income of the condominium. This projection helps avoid potential assessments which are a sum levied on a property, either based on an appraisal or a percentage of ownership in the condominium. All co-owners contribute to the maintenance of the common elements. The common area is defined as the materials and space that are jointly owned by all owners in a condominium project. You also have limited common area whereby material and space are owned by all co-owners in a condominium but are restricted in access and use. A balcony would be considered limited common area. That is, it is common area but used solely by the individual co-owner.

The condominium Fee is an assessment, a sum of money, which is charged to an individual unit or property in order to pay for the expenses as described in the association's budget. Routine maintenance is required for the upkeep necessary to fulfill the expected useful life of an item or area. A Special Assessment is a special sum levied on a property for a specific purpose. So, for example, if the roof has to be replaced and there are insufficient funds in the reserve account, a special assessment is levied to make up for the balance required to replace the roof.

Should it be necessary for the Board to make an extraordinary decision such as hiring an engineering company to solve the issue of water infiltration, a Special co-owners' meeting may be called. This is a meeting of all co-owners in a condominium for the purposes of discussing and resolving special issues which concern the whole condominium.

To avoid what can be unpleasant news from a special co-owners' meeting, it is highly recommended that every association have on file a Reserve Report, also known as Reserve Analysis. This would provide an analysis of the condominium's common property which projects the necessary funds to make repairs or effect replacements. This report acts as a compass for the association and helps determine the necessary capital reserve. This capital reserve, also known as Reserve Fund, is a fund set aside for the repair and replacement of the common elements of a condominium.

Therefore, the budget should include the condominium fee to cover the month to month operating expenses and a separate sum that is set aside every month towards the reserve fund.

Who does the book benefit?

Well, you, of course.

This book is written for the benefit of those looking to purchase a condominium as a home or as an investment for the first time. It also serves as a reference guide for Condominium owners and their Board of Directors.

You may already know a great deal about buying, selling or living in a condominium, or you may be interested in starting anew in this venture. Whether you are downsizing from your existing home, or looking to move from renting to buying a condo for the first time, you will value the helpful information in this handbook. However, whether you decide to buy a condo or choose to rent an apartment instead, this book provides insights which can only help in making a decision that in the end, is right for you.

To condo or not to condo? That is the question

So your Real Estate agent has found the perfect condo in a great neighbourhood for the right price. You make an offer and anxiously eye that bottle of champagne that begs to be popped. Slow down, now is the time to put that bubbly back on ice and start asking the right questions.

At first, it's an opportunity of a lifetime to trade your rent money for equity or to finally downsize after raising a family. However, if you don't know much about condo's and were sold just on what the big signs in front of the new construction sites advertise, you could get a few surprises after moving into your new digs.

How often do I see new condominiums gobbled up by eager buyers only to see, a few months later, the For Sale signs popping up as if there were a fire sale going on. Or, a newly constructed condominium complex whose co-owners have to move out a few months after moving in because of major water infiltration issues.

It's not the buyer's fault, is it? Well, it is. However, "Buyer Beware" aside, although there are usually full disclosure rules when buying or selling a property, many new condo buyers are too mesmerized by the thought of owning their own dream property, and forget to focus on some of the important details, such as the amount of the condo fees, what kind of maintenance they will actually cover, etc. So, while developers and real estate agents do have to provide full disclosure, the buyer is also responsible for making sure that they understand exactly what it is they are buying, by doing their homework and asking the right questions.

This handbook will provide you with a guide on what questions to ask, in order to avoid some of the major pitfalls that new condo owners often get themselves into. At the very least, some of what you read in this book may help you ask questions you would not have thought of asking otherwise. Jot down your notes and or questions on the provided "NOTES" pages for future reference.

It's important, then, to understand the role of the condo buyer, versus the role of the condo seller, and what motivates each one. Simply put, the role of a developer is to develop and sell real-estate property (condos, houses, apartments, etc). Developers typically have their own sales office for new condo developments. Their motivation is to develop and sell their properties in as short a time frame as possible. In other words, time is money! The longer it takes a developer to develop a condo complex and sell all the units, the less profitable the venture becomes. Once a new condominium development is sold out, the individual condo owners are now responsible for the buying and selling of their own individual condo units. That is, Title is transferred from the developer to the newly created condominium association. In these cases, the condo seller could be a real estate agent who represents the owner of a particular condo unit. As with the developer, time is also money for the real estate agent. The sooner the real estate agent can sell the property, the sooner she can get paid. In some cases, the owner of the condo unit may sell the property himself. Nevertheless, his motivation is exactly the same as the developer and the real estate agent: time is money!

The role of the buyer is to make sure that she is purchasing exactly what she needs and wants out of her property. While the laws are changing to make developers more accountable and /or transparent to the buyer, the buyer still has to do her homework, and make sure that she understands the level of quality of the property she is buying, which can be acquired through the hiring of a Residential Building Inspector (i.e., location of the property, building materials used, is it concrete and steel construction or wood framed with brick veneer, pre-fabricated components and overall condition.) Also, what is entailed once she owns the condo unit (i.e., condo fees, taxes, condo Board participation, maintenance obligations, etc.). This is also called due diligence. As the saying goes, "an ounce of prevention is worth a pound of cure".

Condominiums are an excellent alternative for many people who want to have ownership in real property with real potential growth of equity for their investment. In exchange for paying your monthly condo fees you are free from the responsibilities of all of the common area necessities such as repairs and maintenance and general upkeep. Many individuals either switch from their present homes, either because they are downsizing, or are first time buyers looking for their first experience in home ownership. Whatever the reason, buying a piece of the condominium dream comes with a wakeup call which can sometimes turn into a rude awakening if you're not going into it with eyes wide open.

This information booklet is for anyone who may find that, when contemplating the purchase of property, the most important thing to do, is to inform yourself as to what may or may not lay ahead because, once the transaction takes place, you will be the proud owner, for better or for worse.

Once you buy a share in a condominium complex, namely your unit and the place you will be living in, you become subject to the rules and regulations as described in the Governing Documents. Before you sign on the dotted line, it is very important that you ask for the following:

- A copy of the Governing Documents
- The Association's Insurance Policy
- Minutes of the Annual General Meeting
- Documentation on any ongoing legal lawsuits
- A copy of the Financials
- A list of any assessments that are due

- Information regarding a Reserve Fund

- A copy of the Reserve Analysis (if they have one). Many don't

- Up to date information on the sellers' condo fees. For that matter, do co-owners in general contribute their fees as scheduled by the Association?

- All of the above-mentioned items will reflect the true goings-ons of the association's administration and whether or not it is operating harmoniously or not. Investigating these issues may turn up a red flag that you may otherwise have overlooked.

Another very important question to ask when interested in the purchase of a particular condominium is to find out the demographics of those that inhabit the complex. Are the prospective neighbour's mostly young families, empty nesters, and so on. Depending on your own makeup, this will help give you a feel as to whether or not you will feel comfortable living amongst your fellow co-owners. While I am on the topic of who is who in the condo complex, I feel that it is necessary to mention the importance of buying into a condominium complex that you can well afford. Many individuals buy into condos without considering the cost of the lifestyle that goes with it. Do yourself a favour and make sure that you are basically in the same financial bracket, or better than the existing co-owners. This little rule of thumb is a key factor in keeping the harmony of its co-owners. You must be prepared and able to afford an unexpected assessment or a necessary increase in condo fees. Make sure you are in a complex whereby when this should happen, and rest assured, it will happen, you are in a position to muster up the dollars just as your neighbours do. Trying to keep up with the Joneses will undoubtedly backfire. There are many fine wines to be enjoyed. Make sure you choose one that fits your budget and, remember that it is a long term investment. Even if you sell shortly after, you should always buy as if you are buying into a long term commitment. This is a financially sound approach and you can therefore better answer that million dollar question, "Can I really afford this?"

The a-s-s in assuming

Most of the time, buyers purchase property assuming all will work itself out. That the pitfalls don't apply to them. This is wishful thinking and not solely an issue for new buyers but repeat buyers as well, who sometimes feel they know the difference between a condominium and a solely owned private property and therefore are confident that they know what they are getting themselves into. Well, maybe. However, from what I've seen and experienced through my property management business is that many individuals, who are intelligent and successful in their respective fields, end up making mistakes in judgement when entering into the condominium way of life. Not so much because they are not aware of how condominiums work, but rather because they are unaware of the events that take place within the present and or existing association before becoming part of it. Then there are those who are just plain arrogant and do whatever they please to the detriment of the other co-owners and the common area and ultimately to themselves. The attitude being "I bought it, therefore I will do as I please". This ultimately creates disharmony between co-owners and runs against the rules and regulations of an association.

Some co-owners decide to withhold paying their condo fees, either because they cannot afford the lifestyle or as a form of manipulation to satisfy their own interests. Others will vote against any motion which entails paying more than what they are currently paying. Sometimes this is justified but the majority of the time it is not. Let's face it; you don't honestly think that the Board Member recommending the increase also wants to pay more? I say Board Member as opposed to Manager since the decision ultimately rests with the Board. The Manager has an interest in seeing the property properly maintained and in good repair and may therefore recommend increases in condo fees. It is then the Board's responsibility to either accept the increase by gathering a majority vote for their decision, or not accept the increase.

Never assume that because a Condominium is a newly constructed building, it will be problem free. Many new condominium developments have undergone major repairs and improvements due to poor construction. As a result, the new owners have been assessed tens of thousands of dollars above and beyond what they had anticipated. The sad part is that these once happy co-owners are legally obligated to pay their share of the assessment. I have seen new constructions go up and soon afterwards sold out with new co-owners freshly settled in to their new digs only to have major water infiltration damage. The co-owners must relocate temporarily to allow the necessary repairs to take place. This could take months. In short, that purchase ended up turning one's life upside down. This type of thing occurs right across the country. No exceptions. You're probably asking "What about insurance? Are we not covered? The fast answer to this question is yes, and no.

Insurance

When living in your condo, there are two types of insurance coverage's that come into play. The Association's insurance and your home insurance. Just like your prior place of residence, you would continue to carry your home insurance. However, there is a difference now that you have moved into a condo. Your personal home insurance covers from the paint on the walls in the inside of your unit including your personal belongings. The Association has insurance that covers the common elements of the condominium as a whole. For example, let's say that you discover you have water dripping into your unit. You would call a Board member and or the Manager. The Manager in turn would contact the Association's insurer and coordinate a time to investigate the damages within the co-owner's unit. The co-owner must also make an appointment with an adjuster from his own insurer. The insurance companies will determine, according to their industries' guidelines, the appropriate, respective coverage. It's always a good idea to contact your insurer and ask a few questions.

The Association's insurance now has a file opened on the basis of the claim made for damages. The Association's policy will show the deductible for every claim made. Deductibles can be as little as 1000$ and as much as 10,000$ or more. I mention this because one should have a relatively rough idea as to the cost of repairs before making the claim. If it is going to cost $900 dollars to repair the problem but the deductible is 5000$, the Association will end up paying for it in the end. That is, the insurer only starts paying after the cost of repairs exceeds $5000. The point I am also trying to make is that if you continually make claims that don't exceed the deductible, your insurance premium will ultimately go up as a consequence of the amount of claims being made.

The Association's insurer provides coverage for the common elements as long as these common portions are maintained appropriately. Should the insurer discover that the water damages occurred as a result of poor maintenance and upkeep of the roof, they may accuse the Association of being negligent of their responsibilities and go as far as cancelling their policy with the Association. The Association would be Red Flagged amongst insurers. This scenario is not a good one since by law, the Association must have insurance. Finding another insurer may prove difficult and expensive.

Another example is if the Association is found to be making multiple claims of the same nature. That is, water infiltration from the roof every few months. The insurer can actually state that even though it will maintain its insurance coverage for the common elements, it will refrain from covering damages determined to come from the roof until such time that the roofing problems are remedied. On the one hand, the argument can be made that "we pay for the insurance so the insurer should issue a cheque for repairs". Well, that is normally the case. However, we are talking about multiple claims. Why should someone else be responsible for your roof which you allow to deteriorate to the point that damages will occur? Negligence; watch out for that one. Insurers don't cover that.

But wait, let's say that the Association has been doing all that was asked of it to keep their property in good standing. Let's say that a company was hired to repair water infiltration problems and the association had contracted the professionals to handle all aspects of work to reach a satisfactory solution to this problem of water infiltration. At the same time, the insurance company is aware, through ongoing communications, of the Association's steps in rectifying this problem. Upon completion of the work and after some time, the water infiltration problems continue to occur. The Association is forced into a position of taking legal action against the company responsible. The Association now finds itself funding legal expenses. Meanwhile the infiltration problems must be solved. Okay, I'm running off a bit here, but the point I want to make is this:

do not, by any means, look for another insurer to take over your policy until such time that all issues have been completely settled. Jumping ship in midstream reflects negatively on the Association and is detrimental to any proceedings whether they are legal or pertaining to insurance issues. Believe it or not, your broker may suggest that you change insurers as a way to get the Association off their backs. The broker won't tell you this outright but that is the motive behind the suggestion. Don't. Continue until all has been resolved. Then, and only then, continue with your insurer but replace your Broker. Many associations would be tempted, out of share frustration, to go with the Broker's suggestion. Those that do, end up finding themselves out in the cold for doing so. When renewing your insurance policy, ask your broker to provide you with a premium price based on two years as opposed to one year. This should lower your premium expense. Contact your broker two to three months prior to your policy renewal with this inquiry. Also, make sure that every co-owner receives a certificate of insurance for their records. A certificate of insurance is a one page synopsis of the Association's policy.

It is advisable to have the condominium appraised by a Chartered Appraiser. This evaluation is recognized by the association's insurance company and will be reflected on the insurance policy. The insurance company will automatically index the amount of the original evaluation by the Chartered Appraiser on a yearly basis therefore continuing to provide the condominium association and its common area with proper coverage. However, after 4 years the indexation may stray from a more accurate insurable amount due to unforeseen economic and or political factors beyond anyone's projections. Therefore, in order to continue having a true evaluation amount for proper insurance coverage, it is recommended to have an evaluation performed every 4 to 5 years. This practice provides a realistic picture for the type of insurance required. For example, if you have coverage for the condominium for 3 million dollars and the association finds out that it will cost 3.5 million to replace; the association will be responsible for the replacement cost balance of 500 thousand. In short, the report from the chartered appraiser puts the onus on the insurance company to provide true coverage.

The Condominium Association, Board of Directors and co-owners

What is important to understand here, is that a Condominium Association is governed according to its by-laws which are found in the Association's governing documents. The elected Board Members have the mandate, as stated in the by-laws, to govern on behalf of the co-owners. This mandate includes taking care of all issues related to the insurance, repairs, maintenance and general upkeep of the common areas as well as enforcing all regulations, as dictated in the by-laws. All of these items cost money and an operating account is used to finance the month to month operations. Condominium fees are therefore charged to each co-owner accordingly to cover these costs. These monies cover the basic month to month upkeep of the property and its common areas.

A reserve fund and / or savings account is also created to build funds for future expenses such as replacing the roof, landscaping upkeep, repairing a faulty carbon monoxide system and other major repairs and improvements during the life of the property. These are paid along with the monthly condominium fees to the Association.

For example, the monthly condo fee is for $400 + a monthly reserve fee of $75 for a total of $475 a month or whatever amount the co-owners have calculated and decided to charge each co-owner for the upkeep of the common elements.

Now that I'm on the topic, it is very important to determine the correct amount based on a true and realistic study of both present and future costs. Hiring an engineer who offers reserve analysis studies for condominiums is an invaluable investment for two huge reasons. The first reason is that the determined figures come from an unbiased professional source. The second reason is that this method reduces conflict amongst the co-owners. The facts are presented by an outside professional, as opposed to a few potentially biased co-owners. This further develops a sense of agreement, understanding and ultimately, harmony within the Association's walls.

For the most part, people are smart and trusting of others. As an example, when one passes by a new development and sees an advertisement stating "three bedroom condominium for x amount of dollars and x dollars a month in condominium fees that includes everything", one may take it at face value and believe that it's a great deal and fits the budget. That is, you calculate what your mortgage payments will be, plus your condo fees and you find that it suits your budget and you go ahead and purchase your condo, happy that you are now an owner and no longer a renter. Like minded buyers purchase up the remaining units and approximately one year later, the developer transfers the property to the newly formed condominium association. The new buyer is probably thinking that condominium fees should remain low since the condo is a new construction.

Who is responsible for what?

As mentioned above, this newly formed Association must now be governed by a Board comprised of the owners, who in turn, must govern as decreed by the mandates of the governing documents and the by-laws of the newly formed condominium association i.e. The Association was created by a declaration of co-ownership dated Month x, 20xx.

A general meeting is called and all co-owners elect a Board of Directors to govern the Association for its first year. For newly formed associations, I cannot stress enough that these first meetings are very crucial to the future wellbeing of the association. This is where true leadership is required. Unfortunately, more often than not, the bickering and complaining begins, usually about money but also about issues some individuals may have with regards to the compliance of by-laws as written in the governing documents. Also keep in mind that whoever takes on the role of President of the Board, must be someone who can communicate her ideas well to others. This does not mean that an individual with an extroverted personality should be the only choice. Introverts (soft spoken and thoughtful) individuals may very well be an excellent choice to have on the Board.

The Board of Directors, as elected by a majority of co-owners, vote in volunteers to oversee the general upkeep and wellbeing of the Association. The Directors are in charge of all decision making and proceed according to the Governing Documents. The Manager, who is appointed by the Board of Directors, acts as liaison between the Board and professionals, trades and general labour involved in the upkeep and maintenance of both the Association and its common elements and is also involved in assisting the Board in communicating and maintaining a sense of harmony throughout the association.

There is another very important item that we must mention. Remember I mentioned that one might come across some surprises after the fact? Well, imagine a meeting where the Board announces to its members that the association must start a reserve fund for future major repairs and improvements according to the laws governed by the condominium act and will require each owner to provide an extra X$$$ per month. Also, the cost to have janitorial and maintenance work done on the property will actually cost each co-owner an extra $20 monthly. As mentioned before, the buyer who had budgeted for his mortgage and fees as advertised, and who had not planned for additional costs, fights the decision by the Board and votes against the motion for an increase. If there are several co-owners disagreeing, fighting can ensue and usually does.

Relationships turn sour and the chances of ever turning things around on a more positive note are next to impossible. The property, at this very point in time, begins to suffer. If however, the majority of the co-owners vote in favour of the Board's proposition with only a minority in disagreement, then the association stands a chance. Otherwise, it is quite literally doomed.

It is not surprising to see For Sale signs soon after the ongoing lack of harmony. Having a bunch of For Sale signs out in front of the property is a red flag for any prospective buyer and sends a message that something must be wrong. Either the construction has issues or the Association is racked with disputing co-owners. Whatever the issue, public perception won't be positive. This invariably brings the value of the property down. If the value of one unit suffers, it will affect the value of the other units as well. Remember that a condominium is formed by a group of co-owners. Seamless continuity is imperative.

Unfortunately for many condominiums, co-owners are quick to volunteer their time as Board members in order to support their own interests, as opposed to the Association's interest as a whole. A decision to cut back on or eliminate an increase may satisfy one's own pocket book but may be detrimental to the condominium as a whole, which in turn ends up financially hurting the very owners who thought they were making a wise financial choice. Many do not have the foresight or understanding to manage real property and as a consequence, end up doing more damage than good. This is no different from someone who enjoys eating and so therefore thinks he can own and operate a restaurant. It may seem at first that the less one pays the better it is for all, but in fact, the future costs could end up being more expensive as a direct result of fiscal negligence.

None of us wants to spend more than we have to. However, if one cannot abide by the realities involved in running an association, as dictated in the governing documents, and in a manner that increases the value of the property, then the value of all the co-owners' investments will be affected negatively. Should a co-owner decide to eventually sell his or her unit, the expediency of the sale, as well as the equity increase, will be a direct result of how the association, and co-owners, have been governing themselves. A prospective buyer will want to buy into a healthy and strong association and will shy away from any problems that may surface when investigating the possible purchase of one of the units. Let us not forget that the law requires that a seller provide full disclosure when selling a unit. Buyers are now making offers to the seller contingent on reviewing the Association's financials as well as minutes of the Association's annual general meetings. This allows the buyer to back out should, after review of the documents, he or she feels that there are discrepancies and unanswered questions in the reporting. Even if the buyer is intent on buying the property, he can use any discrepancies to his advantage when negotiating an offer to purchase.

In short, cutting corners is the same as sweeping one's responsibility under the carpet. The problems are still there and, over time, become more expensive. Eventually, the truth will become evident. The neglected grounds, the deteriorating brick, the peeling paint, the leaking roof and the list goes on. No one wants to buy a shabby property and if they do, you will end up with a new co-owner who thinks shabby is okay and will bring the property further down that slippery slope.

If you want to increase equity in your property, you need to take care of it while owning it. Some co-owners may argue that they don't want to pay into a reserve fund for a roof that will be replaced in twenty years. However, if you are enjoying that roof now then whoever buys in later should also enjoy a working roof.

Should I rent or should I own?

If you think that owning is the same as renting, you'll be going back to renting very quickly . When you rent you pay a fixed amount and that's it. No surprises. If something breaks you call the manager or the owner and it gets fixed at no extra charge. It doesn't mean you're not paying for it because all of those costs are integrated into your rent. But it is a fixed cost with no assessment surprises.

When you own your place and if something needs fixing, you call the trade and arrange a visit for the repair at your own expense. If you happen to own a unit in a condominium, then the by-laws dictate who is responsible for such an expense and all arrangements and payments are done through the Association and/or on behalf of the co-owner.

The thing is, whether you rent or own, the costs are approximately the same. The difference is in how the layouts of those expenses are spread out over time.

For a renter, the dollar amount is spread out over a long period of time thus allowing the renter to afford the payment of the property he or she inhabits. One's monthly cash flow is then not as stressed especially if the person renting is on a fixed income. When renting, and because one is paying a fixed amount, the opportunity for saving on a monthly basis is very possible as well as very necessary. Necessary, because the savings will be the renter's equity.

For a property owner, one must put aside money for maintenance and repairs as well as major future repairs such as replacing the roof and or windows or any other major renovations. Also, there are amounts that must be paid as they arise for such things as, repairing your plumbing or replacing a broken window, painting, garden upkeep etc. In this case, the money must be available for present needs as well as setting aside for future needs. Also, there are property and school taxes and insurance costs. Many homeowners tap into their home equity to handle such expenses, but that's another topic altogether.

So, even though at first glance one may lean more towards renting, ownership provides the potential for future equity in your investment. That is, the monthly payments in rent can instead be used for monthly payments in ownership with future appreciation of property value. This future increase in equity is for many, the very reason to purchase as opposed to renting. Should you decide to sell your home, you should at least get back what you've paid into your home. In short, owning a home is a forced type of savings whereas, saving when renting is voluntary.

Yes, the main reason for people to purchase property is the promise of positive equity.

Homes, over time, appreciate in value and maintaining one's property may seem costly at first but there are two things where an owner benefits and that is a) You get to live in your investment; you are already enjoying the fruits from your purchase; and b) as you live in your home, it increases in value over time.

Now, I'm not knocking the option to rent. However, if one does decide to rent long term, my main advice is to put some savings aside each and every month to compensate for the lack of property ownership equity. This also doesn't mean that the home owner should put all one's eggs in the basket of home equity, because in the end, even if you sell, you still have to live somewhere and no one knows what the real estate market will be like at the time one decides to move on. In other words, the homeowner should also, as long as he or she has no other debt besides the mortgage, be saving something each month.

So many people buy homes and say that they can't save. Those same people seemingly have no problem spending. If you can't save you can't spend and if you can't spend and can't save you are living beyond your means. "Big hat no cattle", " drinking champagne on beer money," "keeping up with the joneses." Nobody likes to be told what to do with their money. On the other hand, should you decide to join a club, there are fees and rules to abide by. Condominium living is this way. Harmony and its upkeep does come at a price and not abiding by these basic responsibilities only creates dysfunction and eventual deterioration of what can otherwise be a good and harmonious investment.

Conditions to seller when buying

Most potential buyers should also ask for a copy of the governing documents so as to better understand the Association's expectations of the co-owner. It is also an opportunity for all co-owners to review the governing documents and its by-laws and motion for any changes that would further benefit the interests of the Association as a whole. For example, perhaps the by-law needs to be amended to further strengthen the by-law regarding the collection of condominium fees from co-owners who are frequently delinquent with their accounts. This would allow the association to have recourse when collecting overdue fees. There is the need here to have a lawyer who is familiar with condominium issues to make the necessary recommendations and changes to best benefit the association.

An Association will have a fiscal year end date whereby its bookkeeping will need to be reviewed by a chartered accountant to make sure that the Association has been operating in good faith and according to the agreed upon projected budget voted on by all co-owners at the last Annual General Meeting. These records of accounting will provide the Association, and any co-owner who wishes to view the records, with a history of the property's financial and physical health. This information, as well as the reserve analysis report by the before-mentioned engineer, should provide the Association with updates and direction on further decisions by the Board of Directors. Another piece of important information for the potential buyer is to ask for a copy of the Minutes of the Association's meetings, preferably for the last three years. This would allow the Buyer to understand what decisions have been made during that period.

If you are buying a new condo from the Developer, you would need to make a request for all pertinent documentation related to the purchase of said unit. Hire an inspector before signing on the dotted line. Just because it's new, does not mean there are no potential or actual problems.

Does that Manager's hat fit?

A condominium association is a not-for-profit organization, and therefore, the association in and of itself does not pay taxes. However, some associations are large enough to have employees and must therefore file employee tax deductions at source, reporting to the proper government authorities. Usually this will be the role of an elected accountant. Many associations prefer to use outside contractors which eliminates the need of additional reporting and paperwork. This minimizes tasks such as authorizing cheques to be issued for the running of the Association's month to month operation of its common area. The amount of paperwork and time can be further minimized should the Association contract a manager to handle its affairs.

What's positive about having a management company and/ or manager handle the month to month operations is that it allows for a non-biased approach for taking care of the condominium. Managers can also provide insight for the co-owners and educate them on many condominium related issues. Most often than not, managers have a network of professionals and trades at the ready to take care of any issues that may arise. For the most part, they act as a source for taking care of most of the properties' needs. The expense of a good manager is offset by the increased value over time to the condominium's property as a whole. Furthermore, a good manager is hard to find. I say this, because in this industry Managers, in general, are underpaid. Good managers work in this industry because they really enjoy most aspects of the work and they're good at what they do.

A manager also acts as an early detection warning system for the property as a whole. That is, the Manager is in a position to alert and advise the Board on certain issues that may surface unexpectedly and at the very least, be a liaison between the Board, Owners and Vendors accordingly.

There is a lot of opportunity to make good on owning a condominium. Just don't think that all condominiums are the same animal. You might think you're buying a lovely lamb when in fact it's a wolf. Ask questions and remember that there are no stupid questions.

Other stuff

Well, this is the part where I just throw some tid-bits in for good measure.

Everyone loves to feel like they're saving money along the way. So, its winter, and it's time to spread a little salt on the walkways. Unless the condominium is comprised of just two or three units, and you can throw a few bags of salt in your trunk, you're going to want to order enough salt for the upcoming season. That means having it delivered. The order may depend on the weather. Let's just say that if it's being delivered, and you're paying for that delivery, you should order enough to offset the cost of delivery. You don't want to be paying for five deliveries when you could just buy a larger quantity with lower delivery charges.

Next, when you apply salt, there are two things that are important to remember: first, it saves you money and second, your walkways /driveway will be better maintained. Huh? Okay bear with me here for a bit. First, when you apply the salt is crucial. Never apply salt when it is starting to snow. This only melts the bottom layer of the accumulated snow. Therefore, shovelling is more strenuous and a drop in temperature can turn things into a real mess. Icy conditions create dangerous conditions for all concerned. What usually happens when this occurs, more salt is applied to counter the freezing that has occurred thus increasing your overall maintenance and material cost.

It is important to always clear all snow before adding salt. If you have cleared the snow and it continues to snow, come back and redo the clearing of the snow. Wait until the snow has stopped falling and only after clearing the remainder of snow from your walkways/

driveways do you apply the salt. Salt is used as the final step in clearing your walkways/driveways. It will continue to work after the job has been done, melting away the little that is left over making your walkways and driveways safe for use.

Another material that can be spread on walkways for added safety is what is commonly referred to as "pea gravel". It comes in 20 kilo bags and is used as an aggregate in the landscaping industry and can be found in most home improvement centers. It works as an abrasive and/or as an anti-skid preventative when walking on walkways. I would recommend using pea gravel if you have a walkway that is sloped or in areas that are prone to ice-over easily. I do not however, recommend using it on driveways because the tread in tires picks up the pea gravel and brings it into the interior of the garage. If you have many cars using the common garage you will end up with quite a mess. This also increases your maintenance expense.

It is a big mistake to opt for cheaper solutions/equipment because in actuality, it will end up costing you more. A lot more. Case in point; exterior light fixtures. These items can be quite costly and so the initial reflex is to automatically zoom in on the cheaper product: it looks fine and costs a fraction of the price. Of course, you don't want to cash in your reserve fund for the common area lighting but stop and consider a few things before deciding on the cheapest way.

"Bitter darkness away by light here to stay". Okay, poetics aside. One of the first common mistakes when choosing lighting fixtures is to choose them based on visual appeal. Yes, it would be appealing to look at, but the decision should be based mainly on the following: functionality. In other words, once in place, the fixture should perform the type of lighting required for that specific area. At some point in time you will have to replace the burned out bulb. Make sure that the bulb can be easily replaced. There are many models that are pretty to look at but a nightmare when it comes to replacing a bulb which requires unscrewing and removing sections of the fixture before being able to replace the bulb. Losing screws in the snow in the dead of winter? Do yourself a favour and get fixtures with bulbs that are easily replaceable. Replacing a bulb in the middle of winter should be quick and easy.

Shop around for light fixtures. Let your licensed electrician know what you are looking for. Go to the annual home and garden shows. Take your time and choose a product that will do justice to your investment. If the co-owner has to be assessed for the difference in product cost do it and don't compromise this decision to please the few naysayers. Proper choices made on lighting improvements will benefit the property as a whole, lower maintenance and repair costs, and increase the property value.

Choosing the best product for any given situation makes sense. I am not saying that you should buy the most expensive product, I am saying the best product or service for the situation at hand. Plan for it, it's coming and its going to cost you. Why? Because you own a condo and as such you are now part of an Association with by-laws that requires all co-owners to respect the rules and regulations of the Governing Documents. In short, you are responsible for your share of repairs and maintenances of the common areas.

There is one very important thing to keep in mind when hiring a company to do work on the property. Make sure they are qualified and licensed to do such work. The government has implemented strict regulations in this area and contractors and subcontractors who do not follow the rules and are caught are subject to prohibitive fines. The person doing the hiring may be liable as well if collusion between client and contractor is discovered. This would apply, for example, if you the client, makes an agreement with a contractor who offers a better price due to lower overhead costs, and does not follow the proper procedures that respect the construction laws. An inspector who discovers this can submit prohibitive fines that can end up bankrupting the contractor and create a very expensive situation for the Association. As of 2013, fines range from between five thousand to eighty thousand dollars and more. This is a newly implemented government campaign. Any one on a job site, from a labourer to a specialised trades person, who does not have a card or related license, could face prohibitive fines.

Expect to pay more for construction and or renovations because those in the industry must include the costs of licenses and subcontracting to trades with proper licenses. Of course, you can always choose the cheaper quote from the contractor who is not following the rules and face the possibility of paying a hefty fine at a later date. Also, take into consideration that the General contractor is liable if one of his subcontractors is working without their work cards. The onus is on the General Contractor and therefore these factors are part of the overall submitted quote.

Final note

Not everyone is cut out to be a property manager and oversee the month to month operations of property.

You really have to enjoy certain aspects of it to offset the things you don't enjoy doing.

Conversely, Board members volunteer their time in an effort to make sure that the Association and its common elements are governed accordingly.

Having a Property Manager on your side to make sure that your property stays the course only makes sense.

About the Author

Geoffrey Darwent has over 18 years of extensive experience in managing condominium properties and has always tailored his services to his clients' specific needs.

Property Management & Project Management

Insured Bonded & Licensed

Geoff lives in Montreal, Quebec with his two children, Carlo and Adrian.

In his spare time Geoff is part of a motorcycling group and occasionally rides to raise awareness and funds for several charity events. He is also an artist and occasionally donates his paintings to raise money for causes benefitting our communities.

Geoffrey Darwent is founder & owner of CondoCare

NOTES